Nothing Matters but the Sound of Rain

poetry by
Cheever Tyler

The poetry in this book comes from summers spent in Martha's Vineyard and in the Civil War battlefield in Gettysburg, Virginia.

ISBN: Softcover   978-1-5144-7211-8
        EBook   978-1-5144-7210-1

Print information available on the last page

Rev. date: 05/02/2016

To order additional copies of this book, contact:
Xlibris
1-888-795-4274
www.Xlibris.com
Orders@Xlibris.com

The Spirit

The author, Cheever Tyler, began writing with poetry. It started when he lived in San Francisco as a boy. The gentle melody of the Bay and the spirit of the city itself beckoned the passion in the first of his poems. From then on, he wrote his poems when the warm spirit of love crept into his soul again. Later, he began theatrical writing, and wrote three plays, all of which were produced, one in a small theater in New York. He was drawn to writing plays because of the relationship with his characters.

At the end, he wrote a short film that was chosen in four film festivals including a small one in Los Angeles.

Now he is a recovering lawyer with a strong commitment to public service, and writing poems when love calls.

Contents

Cello Music

I remembered the path to
our old house, still small
in the morning mist.
A new door, curtains, and the
impatiens replaced by yellow,
is no disguise for the place
where our hands
had smoothed the daybreak when,
like an arching lily,
you would blossom to your music.
I have been far from
our room with its
lace curtains floating
near the dark oaken dresser
where you left your summer hat
carelessly, for that last day.
A dove calls near the old clapboard place,
unmistakable, perfect and precise.
It was so very long ago, but I can still hear
a cello playing far away.

Rain Sound

The storm came and
touched us in the night,
leaving, snarling
for another appointment.
In the morning,
we lie in a warm bed.
Nothing matters
but the
sound of rain.

Fallen Leaves

We had no remembrance
of the contact
of our empathy,
or of giving or receiving
where we had lost our way.
There was no one,
no thing in which
time was a factor left
on the floor with clothes.
I felt you hurry between
the shadows of the room,
then hold me to be sure.
I remember your gentle shudder,
then the dampness
of silent tears on our cheeks.
The only sound was of rain
on fallen leaves.

A Poem For Peggy

Beauty, quiet, a hope
filling you
with its beckoning
in the stillness.
A gift not known,
but being,
as love
in a baby's smile.
Love coming from your soul
where faith
touches you gently
and where it will
always be yours.

First Class Seats

The early rising sun

gently breaks the darkness;

a golden show through our history,

the majesty repeated for us,

revolving slowly as we

go about the business

of being American, led by his principle, because he knows it,

principle offered to us all.

This day is not by chance, you know;

it dawns for us together, here

on the same flight, on which, he tells us,

there will never be any first class seats.

Dream Catcher

Give me the dream catcher's song
to prolong my immersion
into the light
that comes from the sea
around five in the afternoon,
after a soft air day.
Give me a song,
because light travels
at the speed of light,
and only a dream catcher
can keep it, so that
its thousand instants
can become less than time,
slowing, slowing,
never to forget.

Inner Light

A bright morning sun,
crept with gentle steps into the room,
on this day of late season,
silently bathing things that
I am well accustomed to
in an illusion of an inner light.
It's purpose was unambiguous,
coming here from a distant place
where it had reflected on faces
and in eyes before antiquity,
immeasurable in time and distance,
yet giving me to think in its innocence,
that the visit was made just for me.

Memories

Tears dried in recollection reappear,
barely wetting your cheek.
The touch of your children's hands
warm within yours,
and the embrace of strong arms
protecting you for an eternity,
lie there and there around you,
retained by thin threads
connected to your heart.
Time is time and
there is no other measure,
but the store of gifts
given by many
in the telling of their souls,
memories like petals
floating on a spring brook,
pass by, sparkling,
for you to see.

Blue Boys

The first cool gust of air, then
reds, then yellows
pass by softly underfoot.
Sails, folded into stuffed bags
like fat blue boys side by side
rest, full enough of summer.
Come, the path leads to the bay
where smells of wood smoke
remind us that the great room will be
warm on our return. Come,
and I will show you that
warmth is everywhere
in the October time of this afternoon,
and that there is grace
in growing old.

Lanterns

A ninety-seven year old woman
comes to the podium and,
taking the microphone,
tells the crowd in the Tabernacle
what it was like
when she was a girl.
What it was like in those days
when people would hang
Japanese lanterns on their houses
and sing songs about America
and the goodness of the earth,
just as we do tonight.
The crowd cheers, and all over the square
lanterns blossom into light.
You could sing from end to end.
How about a dance, sweetheart?
It's time we were steppin' out.

An Afternoon Nap

Gently awakening,
I emerge from the comfort
of an afternoon nap.
The old farm is in place as I left it,
graying in the twilight.
But little things have changed.
The sun is soft now,
the hues of lengthening shadows
darkening under trees.
Birds flit noiselessly
but with purpose
from the feeder
to their next stop,
invoking a profound silence.
Little things have changed
but time is still,
embracing me in deep contentment.
The only sound is of wind
passing by with a whisper,
just checking in.

Evolution

Images of people
holding hands,
jumping from the Towers
just head of hell fire,
choosing that little intimacy
before evolution.
What injustice
would justify
that awful, final fall?
Or was it just that
we did not love
or understand?

Old Mirror

Clear blue, the old mirror
like a smoky street light
in deep Atlantis
makes its silent way
into the night,
showing things chalky soft.
On the sea, the old mirror
leaves a silver path, pointing to
the high, cold, dusty source
of ancient myth and wonder.
Its stillness makes us still.
Out in the summer garden,
looking up, the light
touches your face,
and you feel the
delicate, silent,
ageless contact
that now, from a great distance,
reflects you too.

Ancient Messenger

Long ago rolled up
by the cold Atlantic,
the ancient stone
held in your hand
that last day in October,
weighs lightly on my fingers.
Discovered in the pocket
of faded summer clothing,
your warmth, long held within
the Ancient Messenger, returns.
Soon, I will look for you
in other places,
for awhile.

Antietam

Men marching to
sudden suspension
in the cornfield,
feed into the falling machine
that will spit them off
in the first startled
instant of contact,
returning them
in the last rapid red pumps
to thousands of dark wishes that
in the fields of Maryland lie, waiting,
while plumed men on
tall horses
ride among them,
thinning out the herd.

A Boy's Hope

Footprints along the autumn pond's edge
lead to you. The curling ocean
probing the barrier beach, and
tall grasses, waiting, still, in the cool of morning,
hear me say "My father said
good luck follows skipping stones."
So, full of a boy's hope,
I skip you my stone,
barely touching the reflecting steel
until it falls off the edge, exhausted.
After a while, I turn,
gray, and much older now, and watch
the long trail of footprints in the sand,
as they follow you away.

Spring Is Coming

Hearing of you, I walked out
into the chill of November
searching for you in the rush of wind
where you had gone,
the stark branches of old Elms
reaching up for air, waving
at me, resigned.
I remembered your eager gaiety
in Fall leaves still bright
on the dark, wet pavement
that you might have walked on
in another place today, leaves
fading in their last moments
to say goodbye.
I came to tell you that
before long it will be Spring,
life returning after a cold, barren winter,
and to promise that I will look for you
in the rebirth, and the gaiety of jonquils,
where you will be strengthened again
by the arms that held you
in the dark days that seem
with such sadness, to be just ahead.

Eight O'clock Service

Soft rain on the deck furniture;
rain bowing the heads
of gentle impatiens;
rain darkening the bollards
of the town dock,
warming the tranquil bay.
Rain bowing the head
of summer's gaiety, so unaware,
just yesterday,
that one of its colors might be gray.
Inside, at the eight o'clock service,
in the white of communion,
I hear the whispers
of the unsinning
confessing their sins, hoping,
while the soft rain falls and falls,
bowing their heads, too.

Butterfly's Wings

The journey begins
in the blink
of a butterfly's wings,
the shadows cast
by the submerging Roman sun,
soft air, soft eyes
covering us in velvet.
From then, from now,
the interval
is calm and reassuring.
Soft air, we are home now.
Soft eyes resting in the blink
of a butterfly's wings.

Hold On Tight

Heraldic, flaring steeds,
pawing within
a circular gentility,
bearing Sir Hold On Tight,
and Sir One More Time,
voyage out into distant glades
to tilt with the evil baron, Brass Rings.
The mighty chargers
stop now and then
to gather up other little knights
who ride fiercely away, and,
having won the field,
always come home again
to me.

Silver Bells

The delicate sound of wind
combing the beach grass,
silver bells;
your step on the path
coming home,
silver bells;
the shy call of doves
in the garden,
silver bells;
you stirring in the night.
ring as I drift
from the warmth of the fire,
off into a safe place
within old memories,
where silver bells
hang here and there
on cotton.

Soft Eyes

The waiter left her
sitting near a window
facing the harbor,
her white hair wreathed
in the afternoon sunlight.
It was spring, but she had kept
her blue coat on.
She was drinking scotch
and eating sparingly.
There was a distant
look in her eyes
as though to revisit
a place she could never forget.
She stood to walk slowly away.
I remember the place and the time,
and that her features were gentle,
and her eyes were soft.

Safe Home

The ferry pushes through a fog
that covers Woods Hole and the Island
like cotton holding a jewel in its box.
Anticipation drawn out by the
rumble of her diesels
will soon end in an accustomed room
with accustomed things within accustomed reach;
warmed against the chill October afternoon
by a fire in the wood stove, and
the glow of you in your accustomed clothing
sipping warm tea in the wicker arm chair
with faded cushions from an earlier time.
The waterfall of children's laughter tumbling
in the mist and then gone.
An old schooner hauling to windward,
pointing bravely into the fog;
the soft wind giving us motion, and
boats lying obscure in the harbor,
as shadows, safe home.

The Marsh Pond

The thin edge, a line of dark
encloses the marsh pond
as small hawks
graceful and sure,
hunt for life.
The lowering sunlight lifts colors
from the still surface
that beckon the music
of other times such as this.
Each note is perfect and precise.
There is no repetition.
I can hear whispers in the stillness,
fingers touching my cheek.

Closed For The Season

It's raining in Oak Bluffs,
summer's gaiety gone behind doors
closed for the season.
Two warmly dressed children
and an old man with long white hair
ride the Flying Horses,
staring ahead, dreaming,
hanging on to memories
as the calliope plays its song
over and over again
while outside, spent leaves fall
into shallow puddles.
Empty tour busses, painted
with brightly colored kites
seem lost in the gray alley
behind King's Bike Rentals, Inc.
Yellow mopeds
stripped of their youth
accept the rain.
At the end of the street
an American flag droops
atop a small bank.
It is late October,
and it's time, it seems
to be closed for the season.

Lullaby

I hear the melody
of your breathing, and
follow its footprints
into the softness
taking place in my arms.
You closed your eyes
trusting me with
your delicacy
knowing that
the lullaby I sang
to you as you fell asleep,
would follow
into your dream,
too.

Wooden Lobster Boats

Graying shingles absorb
the evening light,
returning things to
an earlier time
when families sang
hopeful songs together
with someone singing
the high part.
Now, my time, this time, is far from
the view from my window, where
an eternity is measured
only by the passing
of old wooden lobster boats
returning home from the sea.

Courtly Men

The Courtly Men loved the Union
and Freedom, but it seems
they loved Freedom more.
Freedom was the right
to have it their way.
Freedom was the right
not to be outvoted by
men who did not understand.
Freedom was the right to
enslave other men to
pick King Cotton.
Freedom was the right to
be forever with like men.

And to get it, they broke the
Covenant, and flung it down.
So, when it came to Union,
the Courtly Men would
give their blood with gallantry,
willing to give more
until the old blood was gone.

And the Courtly Men called
to other men,
and told them the story
of Freedom
and some of them
like the Ninth Kentucky Regiment
marched with the Courtly Men
to war with nine hundred bayonets
glistening on their shoulders.

In the evening
before the last great charge
at Gettysburg, the men
of the Ninth Kentucky
sat close to their camp fires,
and talked, quiet, as in church.
And in the morning,
they rose slowly in the dewy quiet, knowing
that only sixty of them remained
to strike their last blow.

When the bloody day was over
Courtly Men lay
awkward and stiff, their arms
reaching for the ridge.
Only two
from the Ninth Kentucky
would return, leaving
their colors behind.

Then, after a long silence,
the Covenant was gathered up
and given back to the Courtly Men.
And the Ninth Kentucky carried it South again,
while other men in England, business men,
began to buy their cotton
elsewhere.

Freedom was the right
to have it their way
Freedom was the right
not to be outvoted.
Freedom was the right to enslave, and
Freedom was the right to
be with like men - forever.

Gettysburg
April 6, 1999

Clarity

Sitting on the thin skin
of my yellow kayak
I remain above the water,
but a part of it.
In the golden light of sunset,
a fish swims below me, and
gray boathouses remember
as a tern dives, and
the yellow beach curves,
restraining low grass.
I rest, carried by the tide
and a mild wind from the Northeast.
Suspended in the midst
of silence that might
hold the sound of
instruments not yet imagined,
I ask that I may hear,
but the gift is not given.
In the stillness, cool air and the sound
of my breathing remind me
that I will float away;
that I will not remain here.

The gift is an instant.
I am in clarity, and few things
are as clear as this,
for long.

Barefoot

Embedded Emphasis
In the Silent echo
That returns
From the Sound
My voice makes against the wall
Pleading, angry,
So what?
It's up to me now,
It's cold now
I'm barefoot, now
It's night
It's empty
In the house

Morning Again

The soft sigh of a dove
interrupts as morning stops before
the end of my unfinished dream.
You are still lost in the night
when the powerful song of discovery
beckoned us into rolling swells
at the edge of the sea.
Noiselessly, waking you,
I return to the beach,
and carry you again into
the warm, tidal water
where we float in
the heaving ocean,
encased in its power,
crying out again,
to be heard only by the wind,
and the soaring, curious gulls.

Laughter

I hear the laughter
of my children
and my old, comfortable friends
in the room above my bed, playing,
the bonds made long ago
growing as their joy
fills the summer house.
Quit of my solitude,
I am warmed as they are
by the wood stove
comforting the great room.
Closing my eyes
I turn in their company
toward the deepening night.

Give That Man A Cigar

As if by seasonal migration, we lemming
off to the edge of the ocean to get sand in
our bathing suits, sandals, and sandwiches.
My cousin Harvey puts baby oil on himself,
and when he is finished,
looks like a cue ball in a Caesar salad.
Wait 'till he gets sand on himself, I think.
The beach umbrella is rusted shut, and we
forgot the Frisbee. But, floating outside of
the curlers, watching, I like it so much, you know,
I wish I could have a cigar.

A Foggy Afternoon

Fog encloses us
behind windows
shuttered against
a damp gray coat
It is time
for good books,
dozing in comfortable chairs,
and the soft voices
of my children
deep into a puzzle,
here on their summer visit,
coming back to their childhood
and to the memories
that remain
especially clear
on foggy afternoons.

Satin Shoulders

Her satin shoulders a blurr
under tossing hair, she
danced with the
handsome officer
whose gray uniform
would soon come
muddy red
on a little hill
in Pennsylvania
called Gettysburg.
From that sudden moment on,
the dancing would stop,
her hoop skirt
would be put
into a trunk,
and the candles in the
elegant mansion
built by her father,
grown fat on king cotton,
would be blown out
one by one,
for the last time.

The Great Missouri

The white house with its barns
announce the farm,
whose stone walls and
trodden paths have carved
the pastures and fields
where the unambiguous
canvasses of summer and winter
have been painted.
Within, the pictures of Mary
and her family
have touched the old wood,
and smoothed it like rocks
in the brook, over which clear, honest
water has gone down from here
to the Great Missouri,
and in its cradle, out to sea.
Behind, in the white house,
the banister on the curving stair
awaits the touch
of little children's hands,
climbing up to bed.

Rehearsal

The source extinguished, windows shut,
ashes gray in the hearth;
deck furniture like awkward birds
retired to the slowly closing
place of summer's ascension.
I let go as the pulling force
accelerates, and
once released,
grows smaller
on the sea where,
like a steel engraving
my journey is etched.
This may be the last rehearsal.
Surely as I have left things,
light will follow dark, and dark, light.
IN THE STILL OF THE NIGHT

That Old Familiar Tune

Listen to the distant horn
on the sea, the morning
dove's cool oboe,
the trumpet of gulls
skimming under the fog,
and the soft timpani
of rain closing us inward
into a place we cannot see
but know well.
Come, be still for a moment,
so the hands
holding around the
gathering table,
can hear that old, familiar tune.

Light

Far down the hallway,
a door is just open.
Light from the opening
barely exposes the long, narrow space.
Your movements are shadows
that follow you delicately.
I can hear your cough
as I lie in my bed, unable to move.
I reach to you and fold you
into the protection of
my promise without movement,
crying out that there can be
no me without you,
only to hear you cough again,
and see the light turned out.

Pickett's Charge

The Old Tide Raiser with
white hair tired down
called to his boys in butternut,
and in their taught, tattered sinews,
they rose unquestioning
as a great wave
building from the sea,
following his finger pointing
to the high spiked ridge
to the East.
But the land grew steep
as they came, curling,
and the great wave broke,
suddenly spent
in a thousand sighs
crashing them down hard,
the distance from eye to earth
an eternity. In the end
there were only thin, red bubbles
ebbing forward
that soon sank forever
into the high sand.

In the stillness, older now,
the Old Tide Raiser saw
what had happened
and turned away,
crying.

The Bus Is Gone

Through night rain
on the windows
and the glistening street
Greyhound on,
Greyhound off,
Greyhound on,
Greyhound off.
Down spouts pouring alleys
into coffee cups,
mustard jukebox, rain.
The white cup with old lipstick
is solitary.
Don't spin the stool, Mister,
the bus is gone.

The Curtain Falls

At the end of a sparkling day,
the sun takes its bow and descends off stage
on its way to someone's sunrise.
The colorful curtain of sky and ocean
falls slowly in the changing light.
It is silent except for the soft
whisper of waves rushing up the beach
in thin layers of white foam
smoothing old stones in their
long journey home.
There is no applause, but a family
with a small child and a small dog
sitting quiet on blankets
looking out to sea, knowing,
is enough.

Saint Andrews

There is comfort
in the prayers
of the kneeling congregation
in silent rows
on this foggy Sunday morning,
each of us wishing for a deep
and consoling kindness
to embrace friends
and family who are lonely or afraid.
As with one voice we pray,
as with one heart we
unite in that silent moment
in which, without knowing it,
our spirits, as they always have been,
and always will be, are one.

Old Glory

Trying to stay out of touch, I
skim the "Times" after church,
avoiding, staying clear. No,
what matters now are the window boxes
with their red and white impatiens, and
the blue morning glories
winding around their strings,
like Old Glory in a simpler time.

Thoughts Of Chowder

The thrum of Islander's engines
facing seaward, looking,
an old thoroughbred
bound for Oak Bluffs.
On board, sun beats down the expectant
while off to starboard
a red bell sings in our wake
and noble Martha's Vineyard
glides to Woods Hole
on a path of sea foam.
Gulls swoop to snatch upheld crackers
from astonished children's fingers
while the smell of hot dogs
comes now and then from the galley.
A sense of comfort descends
bringing thoughts of chowder.

Yellow Sand Road

The yellow sand road
on Chappaquiddick
curves between green fields.
Made by simple passage
it is traveled, but not foreign,
bending out of sight
beyond the old barn.
As I walk, I know
where it is going,
back in memory
where oxen pulled farm carts
and strong hands
tilled these fields.
As I walk, I follow
until time doesn't divide,
joined by the lowering sun
and the yellow sand road.

Faded Blue Shirt

I got there to find things that must be left behind;
for they don't travel well.
The Album of these images
has no size or shape, but in time, its store of me
fits like the faded blue shirt
left there In the closet.
My pile is carefully
arranged so visits can be casual.
But for tonight, turning the pages again,
There is nothing offhand
about what is there.

A Summer Novel

Clouds have captured
the sunny morning
from our expectations.
Soon it will rain,
and we will return
to the contemplation of
a summer novel
under faded photographs
of a family at the beach.
The certain knowledge
will soon come
that because of this,
all is well.

All You Need To Know About Dusty Sam

One fine morning
Shiny Robert E. met
Dusty Sam
at Appamattox, and
without apology,
Robert E. gave Dusty Sam
a used up dream.
Dusty Sam
put it in his pocket,
and after he had
let Robert E's
boys go,
Dusty Sam died.
And when he did,
they saw
what was in his pocket,
and two men in Gray, and
two men in Blue
carried him away.

A Boy from Mississippi

The Union cannon spat the unintended horror

that for an instant

would startle the boy from Mississippi.

While his body lay still

with a letter from his sister on its way.

No one saw the majesty

of what he had done that summer day

when he began his last empty charge.

High Art

Lilies on the table,
fresh from the garden
dancing gaily
within the slim glass,
so eager to give
their gentle beauty away.
I breathe in their perfume
touching a flower
to see inside the intricate gift.
A drop of its essence
falls on my hand
as if trusting me
in its vulnerability
to remember the last moments
of its giving, choosing me
to say good bye.
I bring it near, unsure,
not knowing that
the mark of it
will stay on my lips
forever.

Gloucester

Shuttered eyes from sea-dark chambers
recall the comfort of light
under a mother's door
and the sound of her slippers
approaching in the night.
Safe then, he cast off
on a whaler's tide
to embark again to sea,
called out from Gloucester
to piping bosun's tales of
Finesterre, and
sounding humpback's chantey down.
But sudden in the cold deep,
the creak of leeward wood,
the scent of whale oil is no more.
And all is still while
slowly, slowly,
a slumber's lifting fog
reveals safe harbor.

Understanding

On the horizon
A golden glow nears the end
of an extravagant performance.
The sea, docile, accepts
the color of twilight;
high clouds float majestically away
to slumber in the night
softly reflecting the last dramatic gesture.
There is a deep intimacy in the silence,
the revolving enormity somehow compelling it
not as a coincident effect,
but as its purpose,
perhaps to say even to one
who is just passing through,
that is it very important
that I understand.

The Dock Street Coffee Shop

Edgartown like an old painting.
whose inner light is drawn out
by the low brightness
of the early morning sun.
The crisp air emphasizes
the delicate selections,
each corner, each edge precise.
Absorbed, I sit at the counter
of the Dock Street Coffee Shop, where
the soft Massachusetts voices are,
men talking about life and the fishing derby.
things and thoughts that
belong just where they are,
delicate selections
of a special morning light.
The paper left by the man beside me,
opened casually,
announces the deaths in Iraq of fifteen
boys from places such as this,
their inner light lost,
delicate selections, each smile
each voice, in memory.

Ten Cents In Natchez

Wall paper
from France
would decorate
high ceilinged spaces
in Natchez
for the new
plantation owner,
suddenly rich
with cotton selling
at a dollar twenty a pound.
A thousand slaves
tilling his fields,
he wintered elsewhere
until the whine of the Minnie Ball,
the tromping of bandaged,
bloody feet,
and the Great Political
Proclamation
drove the price down
to ten cents in Natchez.

Lights

As I lie in the lamp light
my thoughts turn to the last day.
Silver mist in the pines
carrying the scent of the sea;
diamonds twinkling
across the bay;
Starlight heeled high
white to a wind
that held your face smiling
in the high gold of sunset;
candlelight and evening deepening,
while soft doves slept.
Still, in this night,
the old lights return
your footsteps
beside mine in the thin line of surf
and in the long shadows cast
on the dark path ahead.

Porchlight

In a time of emptiness
I have come to this place
to be alone
where I can never be.
By the sea, the last surge of surf
curls, cool around my feet,
waiting with me
for the morning
after an evening rain.
Soon, the hopeful light begins
its distant nourishment
silently asking for nothing
except the passage of time.
A rainbow arcs in majesty,
its short life reflected
like the touch of a summer petal
on my hand to be remembered
another day, perhaps tomorrow.
In the embrace of these things,
I return to the path
and a porch light shining,
beckoning me home.

Strangers

Faces passing by
in the late afternoon
looking at store windows
or eating ice cream,
not hurrying, each
coming in time
to a separate destination.
A few are smiling,
a few are wearing
sun glasses in the shade,
strangers wandering
passing time
in different ways.

Day To Day

Day to day conversation
involving our coincident paths
delightful with laughter,
mimicry, teasing gentleness
that was to understate protectiveness,
absorbed us for the time.
I remember hearing the song,
the voice of a beautiful, ancient lady,
clear and undeniable,
its meaning obscure
until I looked into your laughing eyes,
knowing who you really were.
I held out my hand, and you took it.
You knew, but did not tell
that you had been waiting for me
for a time beyond you.
You put it to your lips, and looking away,
returned my hand, afraid that
day to day should have such meaning.
Some day, if you hold my hand again,
you will understand that our touching
contains a time beyond the horizon of the day
and you will be finally home.

The Train Whistle's Song

In the dark of night,
hear the train whistle's song,
across the fields
of proud Virginia,
where they lost
their freedom
hard won in blood together.
And it had come to this.
So, togther they came
to get it back,
to feel
the sudden shock,
a thousand hearts
pumping boys down
into proud Virginia
where they lay
stark and alone
in the silent
killing fields when
their blood was gone.

And yet, in the dark of night,
it comes back still
again and again
when you hear
the train whistle's song
across the fields
of proud Virginia.

Moon, Moon

The little boy saw the full moon
From his window.
"Moon, moon," he said, as he pointed
Upward, knowing that he had seen
The spirit of the heavens.
The little boy in the Airplane felt
The lift of the Air while he
Dove and turned like a swallow.
"Moon, moon," he said. "Help me fly."
The little boy lay in his room.
The fist of time
Was releasing its grasp.
The full moon shone into his window.
"Moon, moon" he said as he pointed upward. As though he had seen
A spirit in the heavens
He seemed now to understand.

The Red Umbrella

Carrying the sudden intrusion
that long ago
made his perfect
boy's leg,
and the hope
of his perfect
boy's day
into a permanent
limping life,
the bent old man
makes his way
up the street
under my window.
It is gray and raining.
He is working
under a massive
red umbrella.

California Light

The familiar light
that softens California
at Evensong,
seeks out our faces
in the dark wooden corners
of the old place
we have come to remember.
We watch as the California tight
ignites the fields
leading to the sea once again
as if time had been
of no consequence.
It carries memories
that re-enter doors
that closed when
we were cast upon
the paths of our lives
from this place, long ago.
But this is real,
not a rehearsal.

So, come listen
as we tell our stories,
trusting in faded recollections
that will be made pure
as night begins
here, in the waning California light.

Blue Eyes

Gray rocks, gray fog, harbar,
piers, roofs, gray, gray
houses, barns.
Roses white fences,
green arbors, and blue eyes.
What then are the consequences
of wanting what you can't have?

Climbing

Blue, delicate moming glories
scale the lattice,
climbing
to some destination
only they know.
They seem to be
a part of the casual, expected
naturalness of things -
so unremarkable.

Fresh Stacked Cedar

You told me of sounds,

the night mouse's nibble

and the rumble of whales,

the rustle of blue heron 's wings;

by swirl of stars,

a far engine's murmur

sounding through deep water's keep,

and the soft, close rhythm

there in wind blown grass.

You gave me cudding caws,

saft and brown

and an old farmer's fence

to contain their bundled heap.

You told me of a thistle's prick

in young boys' heels,

and of knees in

grass stained recollection, and

of pebbles close to fallen feathers.

You showed me the gust of a storm cloud's
rush to carry memories
over the horizon's red wound.
You took me to dry roads,
the smell of moss
and fresh cedar stacked
by a resting ax.
We walked in the rain, and
you told me that youth is not forgotten.